Some Notes on the Silence

Some Notes on the Silence

Poems by

Timothy Sandefur

Cover by Shay Culligan
Cover image by John F. Peto, *Reminiscences of 1865*
Image courtesy of Wadsworth Athaneum Museum of Art,
Hartford,CT
Ella Gallup Sumner & Mary Caitlin Sumner Collection Fund,
1940.199

ISBN: 978-1-63980-093-3

Kelsay Books
502 South 1040 East, A-119
American Fork, Utah 84003
Kelsaybooks. com

for Robert Hayden

Acknowledgments

The following poems were previously published:

The Ghazal Page: "Apoptosis."

Medusa's Kitchen: "The Ice Storm," "Vacuum," "The Tale of the Keys," "You Say That I Am Poor, But I Have Built," and "Somehow You Keep Exploring in My Dreams."

Pulsebeat: "Walk in Beauty."

Think: "James Holman."

The Agonist: "Migrators."

The Lyric: "Once Again We Fly."

Tule Review: "Relics," "Escaping," "I Don't Need a Myth for Poetry," and "Racine & Laramie Tobacconists, Inc."

First Things: "Seeds."

The American Scholar's "Next Line, Please" blog: "Short Long Story," "Prologue to the New Edition of *The Book of Fate*," and "Pasiphaë on the Simple Life." Thanks to David Lehman for the prompts.

Notes

Racine & Laramie Tobacconists is a small store in Old Town San Diego, California, in operation since 1868.

James Holman (1786–1857) was an author and adventurer who traveled much of the world after being stricken blind.

Sarah Goodridge (1788–1853) was a Massachusetts-born portrait artist who appears to have had a romantic affair with Daniel Webster, for whom she painted *Beauty Revealed,* a portrait of just her bared breasts.

The *Kangi'yuha,* or Crow-Keepers, are an ancient Sioux warrior society.

Cardamine impatiens is better known as narrowleaf bittercress, a common weed. When touched even gently, their seedpods, known as siliques, eject seeds as far as six feet. *Carissa macrocarpa,* or "Natal plum," is a common shrub with distinctive thorns and white flowers that attract bees.

"Apoptosis" is a medical term for the automatic process of cell-death; it is derived from a Greek word referring to the falling of autumn leaves.

Contents

Losses

Introduction

Dubitante

This silence has a sound to it
that seeps between the words of lullabies,
just as twilight circumscribes what
light descends from lanterns.

It fits within the confines of your
gestures. It cups your shoulder like an
officer or a dancer leading. It
notices your slip.

It articulates while making clear it
doesn't really have to, and fingers
your hair with a smile that asks

you how you really know
what's best for you. Maybe it's
in color—blooming scarlet;

purple, even—but its past
remains a mystery, black and
pliant as leather. It's not supposed
to loom above you, but it does.

Vacuum

Vacuum

Vacuum was the same as pressure.
Every day we'd be reminded:
we were sacred, chosen favorites;
just the latest versions, shaped
to fit without a gap. Every
morning, clutching scripts, we blocked
the next day's movements. Every phrase
was finished for us. Every gesture
was into space emptied in
advance. Every night, at lights-out,
the air began to thicken; you would
lie there quiet, feel yourself
being loved, and every breath inhaled.

The Ice Storm

Somehow the ice made details clearer,
carved earth precise; all things nearer

exactness; it made fecund trees chaste;
finished, displayed to be appraised.

A sculpted eagle's wings it glazed
eternally still, and sharp as blades.

An ideal now certain; limned at last;
a paradise pinned under glass.

The Tale of the Keys

They told us if we went, we'd have to leave
our houses and our cars, and have to flee
through lonely forests. We'd abjured their pity,
bit the hand that out of charity
had caged us. But like the carefree swallows, we
alighted at the meadow's edge to link
and weave our glinting congeries of keys
like tinsel straw and sticks in smiling wreaths
to loop about the skinny necks of trees
and scornful busts with eyes too black to see,
and fly toward the woods, unlocked and free.

Migrators

"Into our plaza they come uninvited:
more and still more; all scattering guano;
damaging eaves with their pestilent scratching;
scavengers mostly; probably spies;
if they eat too much rice, they explode like a bomb.
Crawling with vermin and Cryptococcosis,
feeding on handouts and gabbling shyly,
they eke out a living. God only knows where
they nest, in some hovel all littered with hatchlings.
Don't give me that stuff about morningtime being
awash with the angels; they're pigeons and filthy.
Sure, they can fly; feathering smoothly through
aether like light, or floating in delicate
arcs through the heavens; their throats jeweled with purple
and aquamarine, like the scales of dragons—
which they indeed were, an epoch ago, and,
you know, which they still could become once again."

The Tower

Ain't she grand? And tall—by god, they say
she'll top out something like five thousand cubits
high. You can see her all the way
in Nineveh. And all the people! It's
as if they turned a city on its end.
Room for fifty thousand—testament
to Nimrod's leadership. He said "Ascend!"
and we did. An accomplishment
not for him, or his administration
only, but an undeniable
sign of the greatness of our nation.
They even say she's indestructible.

But you should see the arches! Come this way
and—what? I'm sorry, what is that you say?

Three Poems from *The Twilight Zone*

1. Good Living

("It's A Good Life" starring Bill Mumy)

Within His mind is everything; outside
Him is nothing. We're happy deep inside.
Our world is what He alone decides.
All we really need, He provides.

And it's peaceful. Truly. Some have tried
to find some way to reach the other side
of the field. Some of them have died.
Or worse. Better not to play that hide

and seek with thoughts. That's just suicide.
The real problem is your foolish pride.
Stifle it and learn to clear your mind.
If you pretend it's true, you haven't lied.

Most of all, say you're satisfied.
Try not to think about infanticide.

2. The Third Coming

("The Howling Man" starring John Carradine)

Things pent up, things once scorned, we hoped
to persecute no more. We imagined
the darkness of the cell sapped the light
without, as well. And so we pleaded for the

24

Howling Man, and, hoping our new grammar
might unsavage all the superstitions
of the past, or that the center (so
anemic) would be reborn ecstatically
at our new Bethlehem, we loosed him, just to
find that he refused our sacrament.

So then we parsed our hearts—our own!—to find
the final sin, and scoured them in rising
panic, ranting as the circle shrank.
No one was supposed to get hurt.

3. No More Nightmares

("Nightmare at 20,000 Feet" and "Nick of Time" starring William Shatner)

Knowing just what everyone would think
made it hard to even board the plane.
He's been driven to and from the brink,

and he's not sure himself that any shrink
can really cure anybody's brain.
Knowing just what everyone would think

at home was bad enough—they'd all wink
and nudge and whisper, "You s'pose Bob's insane?
He's been driven to and from the brink,

and guys like that are never quite in sync
again"—but *something's out there just the same.*
Knowing just what everyone will think,

he *must* do *some*thing. He sends his wife for a drink,
takes aim past his reflection in the pane—
He was driven to and from the brink,

they say. But he's not worried what they think.
(Down at the Busy Bee, Don quits the game.
deciding what the Mystic Seer thinks
must not drive him to or from the brink.)

Pasiphaë on the Simple Life

(a pseudo-sonnenizio)

"Come live with me and be my love," he said.
I didn't know by "live" he meant abide.
Survive. Exist. For surely it's not living
to be denied what makes you feel alive—
Aea with its lively salons, art,
music, lights. Here there's only olive
trees and goats and work the live-long day,
and maids who drive you livid with their tales
of insipid romances of lives
past. I've told Minos the Simple I've
got to have more, but he lives—
despite his gold and silver and liveried
slaves—an unenlivened life. Dull.
Undelivered. Dead-alive. Unfull.

Prologue to Next Year's Edition
of *The Book of Fate*

Look your name up in the back
and it has all of next year's facts:
stocks and sports; all the stats;
wars and crimes—and all of that
is just the start. The second half
tells how your hopes play out in black
and white. Viewed in pre-post-fact,
they do seem dull. No choice at last.
Buy it, though. It sells out fast.

Hope

Apoptosis

It's when we think we've found the thing we love we're lost.
That's when we find we cannot help but love the lost.

Shadows fall on graveyard frost. They are cast by thoughts
that hover in the sunlight, far above the lost.

You ask me what I think? My mind is full of ghosts.
Thinking of the future means thinking of the lost.

Sunk cost, overhead cost, opportunity cost;
we say "never again," but it's as much as lost.

Glory? Or regret? They're the change that we have left
when we've paid and counted what we've gained, what we've lost.

Our maps can only show us all the lines we've crossed,
like trying to count back our steps. They prove we're lost.

Horizons are the reasons for all that we've sought.
None ever leave Eden. There, what's discovered's lost.

Autumn with its crisping leaves is when life is best.
It's on the cusp we value most what must be lost.

We honor God when we embrace the chance to love;
a gift we live to give away so nothing's lost.

Seeds

(for A.E. Stallings)

Tiny packets of life, these seeds. They seem
invisible in our busy days, and, tossed
by shoes, or cracked by birds, or cast by breeze
among the weeds and stones, they might be lost;
might be scorched, or washed away—or, worse,
bloom in all their grace, and be ignored—
but some of them take root. So words.
They're particles of thought we pitch toward
a generation we can't know. Beneath
the snow, beneath the ash, and still for years,
lay a spring antiquity bequeathed
to us. So plant these in your garden, dear,
and tend them, as Lucretius might,
who thought that all we see are seeds of light.

A Lens

(for Wallace Stevens)

I held a lens against the sky,
and all the waves that wandered in
the darkness came into alignment
as they never were before,

and cannot be again; that lens
with delicate exactitude
carved a place against the night
with its own abandoned light,

and made a thing that I could hold
while all around the wild earth
remained a mystery: an instant
clear like nothing else. An image point.

Oedipus's Hindsight

I learned to garden in Colonus. You think it
strange I love it thus, being blind? I find it
is no handicap. Till Ismene
comes to fetch me in, I often stay for
hours here, watering the olive
trees, feeling their slender leaves
brush my sunburned hands, or listening
to wheat stalks waving in the breeze.

                       Jocasta
loved old roses most, and only now I've
finished pruning them for spring. (I never
mind the thorns, but my daughters scold me,
"Father! Your fingers! They're bleeding!")

                      Myself, I like
peaches best. Their velvet cheeks, the stone
beneath, that promises their fullness yet.

   When I was young I had no time for trees.
I rolled my eyes at old men's platitudes.
I thought the past a waste; a limp that only
skewed my stride. Defiantly I swore
that I would own the earth; that I would live
without a yesterday. Whenever three
roads met, I'd take them all.

                   Now my steps
are slow; I'm guided by the hand—could say,
a third leg to help me stand—but no.
I'm not some dreary hermit. Only now I
feel the prickling light of sun; the dandelion's

feathers; the greyish smell of rain; the cling
of dirt to fingertips; the rattling
of twigs in wind. These coiled roots give life
to fruits tomorrow; they the next. So I
will glorify the land in which I rest.

They say until he dies call no man blessed.
But me, I think he's blessed the day he sees
the twofold joy that's fate we make ourselves,
and learns to hear the morning coming simply
in the songs of birds.

You Say that I am Poor, but I Have Built

"There's no money in poetry, but then there's no poetry in money, either."
—Robert Graves

You say that I am poor, but I have built
you cities whose veins are quivering with gold,
infusing winter hillsides with a glow
that overflows from tranquil evening windows,
and shines upon the sea, now tamed, that once
seethed and hissed, an eternal, breathless void.
In the swirling storm the shadows of the trees
scratch their thin black fingers at the door,
and grin with icy teeth. But I have brought
the child's eyes the gleam of Christmas lights.

You say that I am idle, but I've made
your gardens bloom among the scalding desert
rocks; fountains to nourish the desolate dust;
sown for you wide fields of browning grain;
thickened the orange peel, made the grapefruit
plump and gold. No bleeding slave now scrapes
his grave from the ground for my dominion. Now
I harvest with spinning steel, to fructify
a race that's known no famine; fill your barns
with stacks of wheat and cotton; milk the herds;
press the olive; comb and card the wool.

Yes, say I have no soul. But I have cleared
a path for the peasant and his son to leave
the plains, where only wind once haunted grass,
and raised them steeples of steel and gleaming glass,
whence shines the light of day on Earth's dark side.
Where once they stared across the empty strait,
I balanced a bridge on a thousand metal strands,
and every one I've gilded with a light
that points toward tomorrow through the night.

On the Margin

Birds flirting on the sill—on the
margin, it seems, of the sky.
Here they trip like gentle
messengers, but aloft—
in swarms or spies, or sometimes
loathsome dragons—they flaunt
their vanishing proof, with the flashing
shadows they cast upon the
mesas, or whorls of dust
flung in sunbeams. Life's
alight, you see, and only
feels fleeting because it
is infinity:
a delicate and wingéd
grace that carves the air with
shapes made and effaced
the same instant; always
hence, always next;
just beyond itself,
somehow. And we? Whatever
we may be, at last
we're only memories
of glides and curves cascading;
of orbits, and zephyrs, and breezes
soaring to cliffs in their height;
not the dust but the light;
not just matter, but flight.

Lost and Found

Maybe these are all clichés. Maybe
what a hundred generations felt
can never be our own. Nowadays we
all see what they could not. We know they knelt
at hollow altars, scared of shadows; not
that we've surpassed them, but at least we've learned
the realistic habit. What they sought—
or what they thought they did—we've been burned
too much to seek. Still, I cannot help
but feel it's ourselves that we reveal
more than theirs. They knew what they felt,
forsook, and pledged; what things should be concealed,
preserved, or shared, having suffered things
and earned the succor tested truths can bring.

Meetings

Once again We Fly

Once again we fly;
leaving a scratch on the sky;
patient land rolls by

under silver wings:
black veins of roads, fractured streams
streaked with ice. And we,

lulled by engine-drone,
mark the places that we've flown
on napkin maps. Home's

just the place we're from.
Destination's yet to come—
later. When we're done.

We, now, in airy
ether, grin down carelessly
at ordinary

chores and earthly cares—
in our languid way aware
Heaven is somewhere

below, not above.
Can we wish to be free of
land, law, time, and love?

Still, we do resent,
when starting our descent,
that flight is transient.

Arizona

Another, more candid land,
fullered by the heavy sun
that arcs down every day
in the gauntlet of an ascetic god.

Standing here, it seems at last
that you've arrived at the horizon.
Surrounded by mountains
gouged from the cosmos;
Earth's hot breath,
a kind of weird frigidity
(nothing enigmatic, nothing feminine),
is only space and atoms;
the planet beneath all wrath and patience.

The valley never blossoms—only flowers,
and flat rock facets flare
white, with black shadows;
all fair and pitiless;
all needles and angles;
all facts and confrontations.

Siliques of Cardamine Impatiens

A cluster of matches poised on the tips of
fireless ignition—or blades
balanced on unperturbed points, dully
waiting between the rocks for rain
to come and recede, so they might be whetted by
aridity and patience. Humility
for generations, and so little
but ancestors and aeons to show
for it. Wizened by sun, moon,
wind, the sun again, until
at last the merest touch is enough
to trigger a blast of scattering atoms,
and maybe just one in the spray
will build another clutch of drones.
This dry world is a stillness of cycles
making pointless points again and again;
never and ever the same until
that instant
when something—some stone, or snake, or scythe—
sets thoughtlessly in motion the only
moment that matters, and makes this matter
more. And then the wind again.

The Valley of Siddim

(for Harry Jaffa)

An Indian Summer night, plunging down I-70,
the countryside near Lawrence
a smear in pale beams,
I felt the time beginning to unwind,
and saw the moon, all wreathed in red like magma,
uprise as though to pour a fire on the land
of silent prairie grasses
and the layered dermis of sediments
here and there incised,
that flaked the centuries patiently to dust
while I raced by.

Oh, the majesty of that crimson!
It seemed less like light than judgment.
It glared from mists in starlessness,
in static air, where all was still—
except a shock of white
when predatory wings
snapped and with a muffled shriek
vanished again in stealth.
Meanwhile, trees dropped ragged leaves,
revealing skinny claws;
others, scarlet-stained, only shivered in a wind
that converged from all around
toward the unrelenting light
that once stared down on Quantrill,
on Beecher's men, and Brown;
that haloed roaring prophets,
and shone in lithic eyes
aiming over rifle stocks.

Suddenly the blackness swallowed up that moon,
and I knew that I was going back,
back through testaments of ancient blood,
past Zoar, past Admah, past Zeboiim,
and as I searched the dismal sky,
I heard from veiny, tangled creeks
that loomed beside the road,
the groaning ghosts of millions,
all their destinies flaring up
to some unheard-of crossroads,
then flying past in blackness;
my wheels now were of caissons
careening over hillsides toward the burning cities
obscured on the horizon.
I thought of wrath unpent,
of unsanctified defiance,
of the verdict deserved, foretold,
and disbelieved. And then I thought
of Abraham, who asked,
"Shall not the Judge of all the earth do right?"

Racine & Laramie Tobacconists, Inc.

Tobacco aroma is delicate velvet;
rich with dark experience;
gloomy and proud, like sagacity itself
gazing down from shelves stacked tall
with boxes of cigars, or cases
full of pipes of ivory
and bone; carved exotic faces,
smiling with all their teeth.
Placid shadows part before your
eyes, revealing antique knives
of gleaming steel. You think of rough and
dusty men; their weary traveled
leather faces; wars they'd seen,
suffered, survived. Their fingerprints
were coils of blackened blood and dirt.
They clutched the golden eagles that
they'd spend on lace for brides who hoped
one day for statehood and
for temperance.

Escaping

I tripped into Missouri, parched
with common dust. Not looking for nothing,
not even freedom. That I had
already. Had Jesus' love and my daughters;
my fate, broken in; and the river at dawn,
when blackbirds dart and skip across
the water. I didn't have no mission,
or want to stand for someone's proof;
was proof enough for Harriet
without a world to know my name.
I knew the boundaries, if nothing else.

But the river in the morning sun
reflects its light on both of us,
you on your side, me on mine,
and its judging heat makes our eyes all swell
and tear alike, whatever they say.
Over there was the future rising
rising up, rising north,
rising like that morning sun,
and—no matter what they say tonight—
yes, I think I'm rising too.
I'm gonna wash away this dust.

Keeping the Crow

(Kangi'yuha)

First to the scene of death,
    they'd drive into the earth
their eight-foot spears painted azure
    and bristling with corvid feathers
    that flapped like ragged flags sewn together
from shadows, and tie themselves in place with leather
        strings.

On that barren ground,
    any sound is drowned
in brown grass; the sun pounds flat,
    and water's as far as the stars; an apt
    place to face a final battle,
and stare down Armageddon till the last
        stones

are black with blood. Inducted
    to hazards of hunt and luck, and
duties of trophies and coup, they still stand,
    long past the world's end,
    lances planted to sift the wind
like remiges on lightless wings, for ravened
        songs.

James Holman

He heard the sparrows singing; ships at anchor
swinging against their chains, and the train's
chuff and hiss; gravel crunching under
bootheels and wagon wheels as strain-
ing horses tugged; the grunts and shouts of men
busily oblivious to their
solitary witness. Now and then,
"Excuse me, sir," a hand, a rush of air,
and a man would hasten past on thumping
wooden walkways; then a child's cry,
a scolding mother's muffled voice. Something
changed when sunset came. In the sky,
starlings emerged to tell him of the night,
and on he walked, hearing only light.

Sarah Goodridge

Everything was covered in that dust.
God! father, mother, stiff in Boston
class routine. That wasn't how true artists
lived, at least not men—Shelley, Byron,
Caspar Friedrich—not in Europe, where
she'd never been and likely wouldn't go.
Couldn't pay for school or even paper;
learning watercolor on her own;
hour after hour stained her fingers
black, painting bark she'd throw away;
enduring stupid teasing from her brother
(whose bills she paid). A "lady artist." They
did not *ignore* her, no, and Mr. Stuart
was so kind, but still—such formal praise.

Not like Daniel. He was like a storm
in June with lightning words and cyclone eyes.
Important. And he *understood* importance.
When she told him every artist paints
herself, he took her meaning all at once:
what she sought to say she couldn't say
to men who thought of beauty as above
themselves. They could worship it—but Dan,
he saw that just to *see* was not enough.
She wanted to *be* seen by one man
at least; to reveal herself in clear sun
if only to an audience of one.

Somehow You Keep Exploring in My Dreams

(for Neil Armstrong)

You must be up there still,
Neil, sliding down
that flimsy ladder, bolted
to the lander's spindly
legs—aluminum,
like a jungle gym—
and poised to mess your new white
boots with billion-year-old
silver dust; scuff up some
sand on that tranquil shore;
waving too fast in your home-
movies, making faces
safely behind your mirrored
mask. Your laughter crackles
back to grown-ups in Houston.
Summer vacation will last
forever. Out of sight.
Tonight again, you're splashing
at Buzz in the Mare Cognitum,
or bouncing after a ball
out of bounds, and shining
back our upturned smiles.
Man in the Moon! Hail
Columbia! Peter Pan!
Captain America! Nostalgia
Man! No, not man,
mankind. Host of Daydreams,
you keep flying toward
that earthrise; flinging yourself
at a horizon that falls away
as you approach, around
and around forever.

Short Long Story

I knew the story'd be a little long.
The old man seemed to lose his way at times.
He was in his 80s? Could be wrong;

don't think he said. Told me he'd belonged
to the Air Force—this was at the time
when it was still the Army—that was long

ago. He was young, had never gone
anywhere past the county line
before. Now in Rome—no, I'm wrong;

Berlin? Anyway, he wrote his mom
or girlfriend just a couple lines,
always kept it cheerful, not too long,

not too detailed; told them bombs
sounded like old tractors. He would sign
off jauntily. Maybe it was wrong

not to tell them more? Sounding strong
with brevity? Then he paused, and I
made some excuse to leave. He died (a long
story) shortly after? Could be wrong.

The Mountain

(a lục bát)

Four million lives ago,
under where the sea's slow ages
yawned, a sole courageous
stone emerged, outrageous and stark
to push aside the dark.
A red heresiarch, he rose
unashamed to impose
a new regime. To those who saw
the coming of that dawn,
and watched the waves withdraw, it must
have seemed miraculous.

Since then, the rain and dust and wind
have cut and tried to bend
his will each day, but when the night
recedes, he's still upright
to catch the morning light again.
That gold he will defend.
Firm as the iron in his veins,
he stands above the plain
In confident disdain, for he
knows well we mostly see
inside ourselves when we look up.

Night returns. Stars corrupt
the sky. Still he stands. What can we
repay integrity?
Whatever we can keep our own.

Losses

Orca

She said she liked the killers, with their
black hoods and jagged grins, so
cool. She'd thrill to see them slice through
waves with tails like knives, fins like
thin, upright feathers, too; or
play like kids with corpses on the
icy beach. Chill and out of
reach, all shades and blades, their outlaw
spin was nothing like the sharks
(such desperate, clumsy things) or chattering,
frivolous dolphins. The braves were curiously
sweet to her. Seeing
she was out of bounds, they'd just
inquire, then bending back upon
their shadows, start another wicked
hunt. Careless with their trophies
and their coup, they only borrowed
life, so they could never give her
anything, yet she craved the
way their breath seemed somehow more like
thunder, and blushed at how she felt
herself grow prettier around them, until,
blithe in the night, they'd shrug and
slide away beneath the moon's
mirrored light, and she would stay.

Buzz, Buzz

Honeybee's sweetness hides a golden sting;
she knows a precious, a dangerous thing.
She hides a dagger under a ring.

Want more from life than it's ready to give?
To feel alive, more than to live?
Won't repent; won't forgive.

The sultry heat of Carissa's musk
ripples in liquid red until dusk
when the dance begins; whom to trust?

Her silky flesh is ripe with life.
Her brisk eyes bite with amber light.
The natal swell of hips invites.

Swerve from the plumb and circle around;
thorns like horns all the way down.
Clutch at the clouds on the way to the ground.

Buzz, buzz. The flowery hedge
isn't a boundary, only a ledge.
Life is sharpest right at the edge.

Relics

I couldn't help but skim a fingertip
across the line long frozen under varnish;
stiff, beside a cabinet full of tarnished
medals, the antique man with rueful lips

said it was a German piece. "The repair
was delicately made. Perhaps some fight;
voices clashed, severing the night;
a door was slammed; feet pounding down the stairs.

Careful fingers tried to smooth the rupture
later; reattach the separate planes.
But no mend can realign the severed grain
or knit again the patient tensile structure.

Time has sanded smooth this subtle crease,
now overlooked. And yet no strength reclaimed
is ever without seams. The wound remains,
like every breach of nature's single peace."

Broken In

We came home to find scattered crumbs
of glass on the carpet. You began to cry
and check the locks on the jewelry box, and I
called the cops. I felt my rage become

submission, or a kind of tameness, as though this
opening had closed us in, had reined
us to another's will, somehow. Ashamed
that we had ever lived in such a thoughtless

bliss, naïveté now seemed like sin.
We never felt ourselves entirely
again, or relished our newness wildly,
as before our home was broken in.

We don't think about it much today,
though there are nights I like awake and stare
at the glass door we long ago repaired,
and wish that I'd kept something locked away.

Walk in Beauty

To walk the blood means sensing all the things
that might have been, but aren't; gripping Earth
beneath you like the roots that clutch the dirt
below the trees; drinking time from streams
      that leave you with a thirst.

To walk the line means looking where your steps
might lead next time; it means that everything
can swivel on a single touch; it means
to measure all your words to fit the depth
      to which they'll sink; to think.

To walk in light means knowing where the sun
comes from; feeling that invisible
sphericity concealed by the dull
horizon, and to wait, as dark becomes
      opaque, for miracles.

To walk in beauty means to carry on,
taking joy in giving life away;
to welcome night when night succeeds the day;
to let the stars remain where they belong
      and love them anyway.

Irony Blues

Stars got the blues. (That's why they shine so bright.)
Sun's got the blues. (Burns them out at night.)
Everybody knows you keep them out of sight.

Peace got the blues. (He'll use a chain, instead.)
Grief's got the blues. (That's why he's so well fed.
Gorges till he's fast asleep, then eats some more in bed.)

Truth's got the blues. (The lies were once so strong.)
Trying's got the blues, from having tried so long.
You hear the news? Then, my friend, you've heard wrong.

Dreams got the blues. (Could you have believed
all those promises? Of course we weren't deceived;
when that trumpet doesn't blow, we'll all feel relieved.)

(Heaven fought the blues. The blues, they won at last.
Now they're heavenly.) And Lucifer, he laughs
so sweetly that we'd burn ourselves, if only he would ask.

When the Devil comes, he'll find our bags all packed.
And we'll all hop the train to get our money back
(and spend it all again to buy the blues we lack).

Ironic blues are miles away from fear.
(Just keep your gaze on the corner of the mirror
to save your face from getting a bit too near).

A Blue Sonnenizio

(on a line from Natasha Tretheway's "Graveyard Blues")

Death stops the body's work, the soul's a journeyman.
Still it's never ready for that final journey, man.
To cross the line of days and nights, into Forever Land.

When he comes to summon you, you'll lay aside your work.
You pretend it never ends, but that'll never work.
Mister Death can wait the hour, never bores or shirks.

He drops another minute on the scale of your body.
He'll weigh you down eventually, you and everybody.
Don't try to beg or hide from him, or bribe him with your money.

He's gonna take you with him when he makes his midnight stop.
Mister Death will come for you when *he* decides to stop.
He knows your weeks and months will pass. You can't outwait his
        clock.

Watching you as you slow down, his wheels, they still roll.
Soon he'll start his journey to Forever with your soul.

I Don't Need a Myth for Poetry

I just need a wave of tiny photons
born in seething plasma filaments
blasted from the surfaces of suns
so far away they almost seem to be
countless little particles of light
racing at the speed of time through frigid
folds of weird eternity until
a thousand generations later, Earth
will weave them into pink and turquoise veils,
singing among the stars of northern skies,

or, ending that immeasurable journey,
fall through the lensing atmosphere
to crash on the surfaces of leaves,
igniting autumn's furious and silent
burn; red and gold, they spin, and then
they fall in curling wind; and in fields,
once again, they yield their energy.

About the Author

Timothy Sandefur is an attorney and writer in Phoenix, Arizona. His books include *The Permission Society* (2016), *Frederick Douglass: Self Made Man* (2018) and *The Ascent of Jacob Bronowski: The Life and Ideas of a Popular Science Icon* (2019).